The Art of Cupcakes

Designed by Michal and Dekel
Layout by Ariane Rybski
Edited by Shoshana Brickman
Photography by Danya Weiner

STERLING and the distinctive Sterling logo are registered trademarks of
Sterling Publishing Co., Inc.

Library of Congress Cataloging-in-Publication Data Available

2 4 6 8 10 9 7 5 3 1

Published by Sterling Publishing Co., Inc.
387 Park Avenue South, New York, NY 10016
© 2010 by Penn Publishing Ltd.
Distributed in Canada by Sterling Publishing
c/o Canadian Manda Group, 165 Dufferin Street
Toronto, Ontario, Canada M6K 3H6
Distributed in the United Kingdom by GMC Distribution Services
Castle Place, 166 High Street, Lewes, East Sussex, England BN7 1XU
Distributed in Australia by Capricorn Link (Australia) Pty. Ltd.
P.O. Box 704, Windsor, NSW 2756, Australia

Printed in China
All rights reserved

Sterling ISBN 978-1-4027-5900-0

For information about custom editions, special sales, premium and
corporate purchases, please contact Sterling Special Sales
Department at 800-805-5489 or specialsales@sterlingpublishing.com.

The Art of Cupcakes

More Than 40 Festive Recipes

Noga Hitron

Photography by Danya Weiner

STERLING

New York / London
www.sterlingpublishing.com

Introduction 6

Basic Recipes 7

Basic Techniques 10

How to Use This Book 11

Tools and Materials 12

Cupcake Designs

All in the Family...........................14

Smiling Mom 16

Delighted Dad 18

Boy Oh Boy!................................20

Girl of Your Dreams 22

Doggone It! 24

What a Wedding!.......................26

Celebrate in Silver 28

Heart-to-Heart..............................30

Big-Hearted Cupcake 32

Miniature Wedding Cake 34

Elegant Paper Waves 36

In the Garden 38

Dainty Daisy 40

Private Garden 42

Freshly Picked Flower........................44

Field of Flowers 46

Springtime Blossoms 48

A Multitude of Monsters...............50

Blue Monster................................52

Green Monster 54

Purple Monster..............................56

Pink Monster................................58

Orange Monster 60

Yellow Monster..............................62

The Wild Ones...........................64

Mischievous Monkey.........................66

Lovable Lion................................68

Very Happy Hippo 70

A Tiger's Tale 72

Positively Panda 74

Celebrating Baby 76

Cute as a Bunny 78

Pacifier, Please 80

Baby Booty 82

Bear on Bib 84

Baby Face...................................86

Teddy Bear 88

Happy Birthday..........................90

Say It with Cupcakes!........................92

Lucky Lollipop 94

How Old Are You?!...........................96

Here Come the Clowns.......................98

Gallery of Gifts.............................101

Fun in the Sun...........................104

Something Fishy............................106

Perfect Weather 108

Bathing Beauty.............................110

You're a Lifesaver 112

Beach Umbrella............................114

Templates 117

Index...................................128

Introduction

Cupcakes are precious parcels of cake that fit perfectly into the palm of one's hand. Dressed up and decorated, they are ideal desserts for any occasion. They can be elegant and formal, silly and playful, or sweet and adorable. They can be served at baby showers or weddings, children's parties or family get-togethers. Since you don't need knives or forks to eat them, they are excellent for bringing to picnics and bake sales, and serving at occasions when minimizing fuss is important.

Cupcakes aren't just miniature cakes, though. They actually have several benefits over cakes. If this is your first time decorating with rolled fondant, you'll probably find it easier to tackle a tiny cupcake design than to embark on decorating a cake. As for preparing the batter, the recipes in this book are easy to follow and use just one bowl! Cupcakes require little baking time and are excellent for freezing. It's easy to estimate how many cupcakes you'll need for your occasion, too. Just count the number of guests, and make sure you have at least one cupcake for each.

The Art of Cupcakes contains more than 40 unique cupcake designs using rolled fondant. The designs are divided into 8 sections, and you are free to mix and match designs at will. For example, you may decide to make a variety of Clowns (page 98) for a birthday party, or make a few of these cupcakes and a couple of Lollipops (page 94) as well. You can make all of the designs in a single section, or several identical cupcakes. You can design the cupcakes exactly as they are described and photographed in this book, or personalize them to suit your occasion.

Basic Recipes

These one-bowl recipes are easy to make and delicious. They also freeze beautifully, so if you only need half a batch, consider baking a full batch and freezing the extras (for up to 2 months) in an airtight container.

Chocolate Cupcakes

Makes 40 standard cupcakes or 20 large cupcakes

Ingredients

5 ounces (142 grams) bittersweet chocolate, melted

1 cup (200 grams) butter, at room temperature

3 large eggs

1¾ cups (350 grams) sugar

1¾ cups (350 grams) all-purpose flour

2 teaspoons (10 grams) baking powder

5 heaping tablespoons (35 grams) unsweetened cocoa powder

1 cup (250 ml) boiling water

1 cup (250 ml) chocolate chips

Instructions

1. Preheat oven to 350°C (180°C).

2. In a large bowl, mix together chocolate and butter until smooth.

3. Add eggs and mix until smooth. Add sugar, flour, baking powder, and cocoa. Stir until evenly mixed.

4. Add boiling water and chocolate chips, and mix until smooth.

5. Spoon batter into baking cups until ⅔ full. Bake for about 15 minutes, or until firm to the touch. Transfer to a wire rack to cool.

White Cupcakes

Makes 40 standard cupcakes or 20 large cupcakes

Ingredients

4 large eggs

1½ cups (300 grams) sugar

½ cup (125 ml) oil

¾ cup (200 ml) orange juice

2 cups (260 grams) self-rising flour

Instructions

1. Preheat oven to 350°F (180°C).

2. In the bowl of an electric mixer, whip together eggs and sugar until light and fluffy.

3. Mix in oil and orange juice, alternating with flour, and mix until smooth.

4. Spoon batter into baking cups until ⅔ full. Bake for about 15 minutes, or until firm to the touch. Transfer to a wire rack to cool.

Buttercream

Use this sweet frosting to cover cupcakes and provide a smooth surface for applying rolled fondant. You can also use jam, chocolate spread, or marzipan to frost cupcakes before decorating.

Makes 3 cups (750 ml)

Ingredients

1 cup (200 grams) butter, at room temperature

1 teaspoon (5 ml) vanilla extract

4 cups (440 grams) sifted confectioners' sugar

2 tablespoons (30 ml) milk

Instructions

1. Place butter in bowl of electric mixer and cream. Add vanilla and mix well. Gradually sift sugar into bowl, 1 cup at a time, while beating at medium speed. Scrape sides and bottom of bowl often. When all of the sugar has been added, icing will appear dry.

2. Add milk, and beat at medium speed until light and fluffy. Use immediately, or transfer to an airtight container and refrigerate for up to two weeks. Re-whip before using.

Rolled Fondant

Also known as sugarpaste, this soft and smooth icing can be purchased at baking supply stores or made at home. Plain rolled fondant is a whitish color, but it is easily tinted with gel food coloring (page 10). Rolled fondant can also be purchased in a wide range of ready-made colors.

Makes 2 pounds (900 grams)

Ingredients

1 tablespoon (15 grams) unflavored gelatin

3 tablespoons (45 ml) cold water

½ cup (125 ml) liquid glucose

1 tablespoon (15 ml) glycerin

2 tablespoons (25 grams) solid vegetable shortening

8 cups (880 grams) sifted confectioners' sugar

Instructions

1. Put gelatin in water and let stand until thick. Place gelatin mixture in top of double boiler and heat gently until gelatin dissolves. Add glucose and glycerin, and mix well. Stir in shortening and remove from heat just before shortening melts completely. Allow mixture to cool slightly.

2. In a large bowl, place 4 cups (440 grams) sugar, and make a well in center. Pour gelatin mixture into well and stir, mixing until no longer sticky.

3. Add remaining 4 cups (440 grams) sugar, kneading until mixture doesn't stick to your hands. Transfer to an airtight container and store in a cool, dry place until ready to use. Do not refrigerate or freeze.

Modeling Paste (Rolled Fondant with CMC)

Adding a thickening agent to rolled fondant makes it malleable for modeling and sturdier for making large shapes. Carboxyl Methyl Cellulose (CMC) and tragacanth gum are two types of edible thickening agents used for this purpose. CMC is cheaper than tragacanth gum and can be stored longer.

Makes 1 pound (454 grams)

Ingredients

Cornstarch, for dusting

2 teaspoons (10 ml) CMC or tragacanth gum

1 pound (454 grams) rolled fondant

Instructions

1. Dust a dry surface with cornstarch and sprinkle CMC over top. Place rolled fondant on CMC and knead until smooth.

2. Transfer to an airtight container and store for at least 1 hour before use. Store in a cool, dry place until ready to use. Do not refrigerate or freeze.

Royal Icing

Royal icing is used to pipe decorations in some designs, and it can also be used as glue for adding ribbons or other items to your cupcakes. Royal icing can be made with fresh egg whites or meringue powder.

Royal Icing (with fresh egg whites)

Makes 1½ cups (375 ml)

Ingredients

1 large egg white

1½ cups (165 grams) sifted confectioners' sugar

1 tablespoon (15 ml) water

Instructions

1. Place egg white and sugar in bowl of electric mixer and mix on low speed for about 10 minutes, or until thick and creamy.

2. Test consistency by lifting some icing with a spoon. If icing holds a soft peak for 10 seconds, it's the right consistency. Add water to thin or sugar to thicken, as necessary.

3. Store in an airtight container until ready to use.

Royal Icing (with meringue powder)

Makes 1½ cups (375 ml)

Ingredients

2 tablespoons (30 ml) water

1 tablespoon (15 grams) meringue powder

1½ cups (165 grams) sifted confectioners' sugar

Instructions

1. Place water and meringue powder in bowl and mix until powder is completely dissolved and mixture is free of lumps.

2. Transfer to bowl of electric mixer. Add sugar and mix on low speed for about 10 minutes, or until thick and creamy.

3. Test consistency by lifting some icing with a spoon. If icing holds a soft peak for 10 seconds, it's the right consistency. Add water to thin or sugar to thicken, as necessary.

4. Store in an airtight container until ready to use.

Basic Techniques

Adding gel food coloring

- Rolled fondant and modeling paste can be purchased in a variety of colors. But if you prefer to do the tinting yourself, I recommend using gel food coloring.

- Gel food coloring is nontoxic, doesn't leave an aftertaste, and comes in a wide variety of rich, vibrant colors. To use, dip a toothpick into the food coloring, and add to rolled fondant. Knead until evenly blended. If necessary, add a little more food coloring and knead again. Continue until you achieve the desired shade. You may want to wear gloves when kneading, since the color can stain your hands.

- If possible, add food coloring to rolled fondant before adding CMC (see page 8) to make modeling paste, since rolled fondant is easier to knead. The addition of CMC will cause colors to fade a bit, so keep this mind as you tint.

Working with rolled fondant and modeling paste

- Always work on a dry surface lightly covered with cornstarch.

- If your rolled fondant is a bit too hard, try heating it in the microwave for a few seconds. Do not overheat!

- If you find the rolled fondant isn't stable enough to hold the shapes you're sculpting, try adding a little CMC.

- Tightly wrap any leftover rolled fondant and modeling paste. When stored in an airtight container and kept in a cool, dry place, rolled fondant and modeling paste can last for several months. Do not refrigerate or freeze.

- If you are working with a really thin sheet of rolled fondant, keep it covered with plastic wrap. This prevents the rolled fondant from hardening as you work.

- In almost all cases, you can affix rolled fondant pieces by simply rubbing a little water on the area (with your fingers or a paintbrush). If you have trouble getting the pieces to stick (perhaps because they dried during handling), trying using a little royal icing as glue.

How to Use This Book

The instructions in almost every project explain how to make one cupcake. You may choose to make several cupcakes in the same design, or several different designs from the same chapter. Here are some tips to help you plan your cupcakes.

1. Make a list of the designs you plan to make. You may want to choose designs from a single chapter, or mix and match designs from several chapters.

2. Make a list of the colors and quantities of rolled fondant you'll need. Many projects require very small amounts of each color. By calculating the total amount you'll need for all colors right at the beginning, you'll save preparation time in every project.

3. Prepare for leftovers. The quantities suggested in this book are generous estimates. Working with small quantities is difficult, especially when adding color. Furthermore, it is much better to be left with too much rolled fondant or modeling paste than too little! Carefully wrap up leftovers and store in a cool, dry place until your next decorating project.

4. Read the instructions from start to finish before beginning. Some designs require you to make parts several hours in advance, so plan carefully.

5. Distinguish between small amounts and tiny amounts. In some cases, the amount of rolled fondant and modeling paste required for a single design is simply too small to measure. In these cases, the terms "small amount" and "tiny amount" are used. A small amount is less than $1/13$ ounce (2 grams); a tiny amount is less than $1/25$ ounce (1 gram).

6. All of the designs are for standard 3 ½-inch (8.9 cm) cupcakes, unless otherwise stated. Of course, you may make choose to make your cupcakes larger or smaller.

7. Prepare cupcakes properly before icing. Make sure cupcakes are completely cooled before decorating. Level tops with a serrated knife, and, using a small spatula, spread enough buttercream to affix rolled fondant.

8. Remove non-edible items before serving. Several designs use pieces of dry spaghetti, wire, lollipop sticks, and ribbon. Please make sure these non-edible items are removed before cupcakes are eaten.

9. Store decorated cupcakes in a dry, cool place that is away from direct heat or sunlight. Do not refrigerate or freeze.

Tools and Materials

All of the tools used in these projects can be found in specialty baking shops or online. Feel free to substitute any of the tools with items in your kitchen. For example, if you don't have a pastry tip that is just the right size for making fish scales (page 106), try using a drinking straw that has been cut in half.

Baking cups All of the designs in this book are prepared in white paper cups, unless otherwise stated. Feel free to adjust your baking cups according to the design you choose and the selection in your store (Figures A to D).

Ball tools are round-headed. They come in many sizes and are used to indent rolled fondant. If you have only a small ball tool, move it around to make the indent as large as you like (Figure E).

Bone tools are used to indent rolled fondant and modeling paste. A paintbrush handle can be used instead (Figure F).

Clay gun is used to press strands of rolled fondant into distinct shapes (Figure G).

Cutters are used to cut flowers, circles, stars, and other shapes. Glass cups, plates, baking pans, and templates can also be used (Figure H).

Decorating bags and tips are used to pipe royal icing. Decorating tips can also be used to make small round indents.

Design wheelers are used to create seamed lines in rolled fondant (Figure I).

Drinking straws are used as a base for drying rolled fondant in an arc, and for indenting small circles and semicircles.

Floral wire is used to support flowers and other shapes.

Food coloring pens can be used to draw details on rolled fondant or modeling paste.

Lollipop sticks are used to support umbrellas and other decorations.

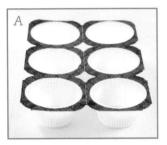

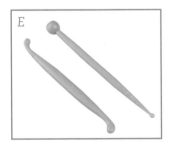

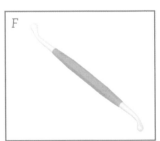

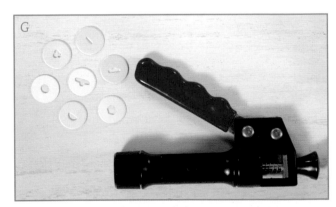

Open-curve crimper is used to create textured trims around edges (Figure J).

Paintbrushes are used to apply water for affixing rolled fondant and modeling paste (Figure K).

Pieces of dry spaghetti are used as supports for horns, arms, and other objects made from rolled fondant.

Pieces of sponge are useful for supporting pieces as they dry.

Pizza cutters are used to cut long, straight strips of rolled fondant.

Plastic wrap is used to cover sheets of rolled fondant to prevent them from drying as you work.

Ribbon is used to add accents to several designs.

Rolling pins (Figure L) are used for rolling out rolled fondant or modeling paste. **Lined rolling pins** (Figure M) and **spiral rolling pins** (Figure N) create textured surfaces.

Serrated knives are used to level the tops of cupcakes.

Small sharp knives are used to cut rolled fondant according to templates, or to add detail.

Small spatulas are used to spread frosting on cupcakes before covering with rolled fondant (Figure O).

Toothpicks used to make tiny indents. Be sure to use high-quality, rounded toothpicks that don't splinter.

Wooden skewers are used to poke holes.

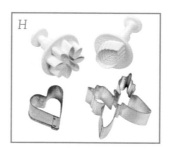

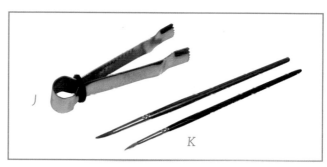

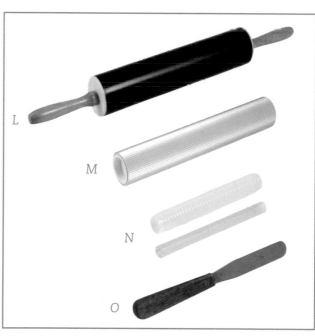

All in the Family

Smiling Mom

A

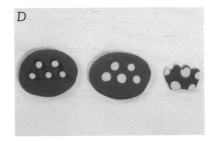

D

B

E

C

Materials

1 cupcake

1 teaspoon (5 ml) buttercream or other spread

Rolled fondant in the following colors:

• 2¹/₂ ounces (70 grams) flesh-colored

• Tiny amount red

• Tiny amount dark brown

• ¹/₄ ounce (7 grams) pink

• Small amount yellow

• 1 ounce (28 grams) brown

Water

Tools

Serrated knife

Small spatula

Rolling pin

3-inch (7.5 cm) round cutter

Small sharp knife

Toothpick

Small ball tool

Bone tool

Small piece of sponge

Instructions

1. Level top of cupcake, and spread buttercream evenly on top. Roll out flesh-colored rolled fondant and cut disc with round cutter. Set aside scraps for nose and ears. Cut U-shaped mouth (**Figure A**). Lay disc on cupcake and press gently to secure.

2. To make cheeks, press mouth up at both ends with toothpick. Make indents for eyes using ball tool. Divide leftover flesh-colored rolled fondant into three even pieces. Shape one piece into a thin triangular nose and affix. Shape other two pieces into oval ears, indent with bone tool, and affix (**Figure B**).

3. Shape red rolled fondant into lips, and affix on mouth. To make eyes, roll two even balls of dark brown rolled fondant, and affix into indents (**Figure C**).

4. To make collar, roll out pink rolled fondant. Roll several small balls of yellow rolled fondant, arrange on pink rolled fondant, and roll gently to inlay. Cut collar using template on page 117 (**Figure D**). Affix collar and support with piece of sponge until dry.

5. To make hair, set aside a little brown rolled fondant for bangs and eyebrows. Shape remaining brown rolled fondant into two even sausage shapes long enough to extend from top of cupcake to below ears. Curl ends of sausage shapes outward and affix. Make two small cones of brown rolled fondant for bangs and affix. Make two tiny cones for eyebrows and affix (**Figure E**).

Delighted Dad

Materials

1 cupcake

A little buttercream, or other spread

Rolled fondant in the following colors:

- $2^{1}/_{2}$ ounces (70 grams) flesh-colored
- Tiny amount red
- 1 ounce (28 grams) brown
- Small amount black

Water

Tools

Serrated knife

Small spatula

Rolling pin

3-inch (7.5 cm) round cutter

Small sharp knife

Toothpick

Small ball tool

Bone tool

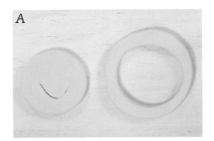

A

B

C

D

E

Instructions

1. Level top of cupcake, and spread buttercream evenly on top. Roll out flesh-colored rolled fondant, and cut disc with round cutter. Set aside scraps for nose and ears. Cut moon-shaped mouth (**Figure A**). Lay disc on cupcake and press gently to secure.

2. To make cheeks, press mouth up at both ends with toothpick. Make indents for eyes using ball tool. Divide leftover flesh-colored rolled fondant into three even pieces. Shape one piece into a triangular nose and affix. Shape other two pieces into oval ears, indent with bone tool, and affix (**Figure B**).

3. Roll red rolled fondant into a thin sausage shape that tapers at both ends, and affix inside mouth. To make eyes, roll two small balls of brown rolled fondant, and affix into indents (**Figure C**).

4. To make eyebrows, roll two small cones of brown rolled fondant, and affix. To make hair, shape remaining brown rolled fondant into seven even sausage shapes. Gently flatten each sausage shape and affix along top of head.

5. To make bowtie, roll out black rolled fondant, cut using template on page 117 (**Figure D**), and affix (**Figure E**).

Boy Oh Boy!

Boys of any age will be thrilled to get a personalized bite-sized cake.

A

B

C

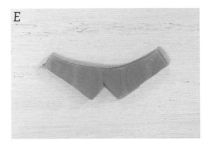
D

E

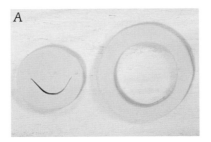
F

Materials

1 cupcake

1 teaspoon (5 ml) buttercream or other spread

Rolled fondant in the following colors:

• 2$^{1}/_{2}$ ounces (70 grams) flesh-colored

• Tiny amount red

• Tiny amount dark brown

• $^{1}/_{2}$ ounce (14 grams) blue

• Small amount green

• 1 ounce (28 grams) brown

Water

Tools

Serrated knife

Small spatula

Rolling pin

3-inch (7.5 cm) round cutter

Small sharp knife

Toothpick

Small ball tool

Bone tool

Small piece of sponge

Instructions

1. Level top of cupcake, and spread buttercream evenly on top. Roll out flesh-colored rolled fondant, and cut disc with round cutter. Set aside scraps for nose and ears. Cut moon-shaped mouth (**Figure A**). Lay disc on cupcake and press gently to secure.

2. Press mouth up at both ends with toothpick to make cheeks. Make indents for eyes using ball tool. Divide leftover flesh-colored rolled fondant into three even pieces. Shape one piece into an oval nose and affix. Shape other two pieces into oval ears, indent with bone tool, and affix (**Figure B**).

3. Roll red rolled fondant into a thin sausage shape that tapers at both ends, and affix inside mouth. To make eyes, roll two small balls of dark brown rolled fondant, and affix into indents (**Figure C**).

4. To make collar, roll out blue rolled fondant. Roll several small sausage shapes of green rolled fondant, lay in stripes on blue rolled fondant, and roll gently to inlay. Cut collar using template on page 117 (**Figures D and E**). Affix collar and support with piece of sponge until dry.

5. Roll a tiny cone of brown rolled fondant for eyebrow. Roll out remaining brown rolled fondant, cut hair using template on page 118, and affix (**Figure F**).

Girl of Your Dreams

A

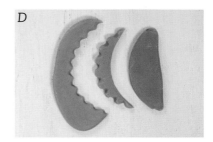

D

B

E

C

Materials

1 cupcake

1 teaspoon (5 ml) buttercream or other spread

Rolled fondant in the following colors:

• 2$\frac{1}{2}$ ounces (70 grams) flesh-colored

• Tiny amount red

• Tiny amount blue

• $\frac{1}{2}$ ounce (14 grams) purple

• Tiny amount orange

• 1 ounce (28 grams) yellow

Water

Tools

Serrated knife

Small spatula

Rolling pin

3-inch (7.5 cm) plain round cutter

Small sharp knife

Toothpick

Small ball tool

3-inch (7.5 cm) fluted round cutter

Small piece of sponge

Instructions

1. Level top of cupcake, and spread buttercream evenly on top. Roll out flesh-colored rolled fondant, and cut disc with plain round cutter. Set aside scraps for nose. Cut moon-shaped mouth (**Figure A**). Lay disc on cupcake and press gently to secure.

2. Press mouth up at both ends with toothpick to make cheeks. Use leftover flesh-colored rolled fondant to shape an oval nose, and affix. Make indents for eyes using ball tool (**Figure B**).

3. Roll red rolled fondant into a thin sausage shape that tapers at both ends, and affix inside mouth. Roll two small balls of blue rolled fondant for eyes, and affix into indents (**Figure C**).

4. To make collar, roll out purple rolled fondant. Cut outside edge of collar with fluted round cutter, and inside edge with plain round cutter (**Figure D**). Affix collar and support with piece of sponge until dry. Roll a tiny ball of orange rolled fondant and a tinier ball of yellow rolled fondant. Affix yellow ball to orange ball, and affix orange ball to center of collar.

5. To make hair, roll out remaining yellow rolled fondant. Cut two sections of hair using template on page 118 (turn template over for second hair section), and affix (**Figure E**).

Doggone It!

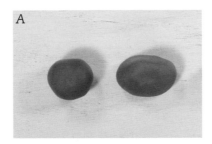

A

D

B

E

C

Materials

1 cupcake

1 teaspoon (5 ml) buttercream or other spread

Rolled fondant in the following colors:

• 3¼ ounces (91 grams) brown

• ⅔ ounce (19 grams) dark brown

• Small amount black

• Tiny amount red

Water

Tools

Serrated knife

Small spatula

Rolling pin

3-inch (7.5 cm) round cutter

Small sharp knife

Bone tool

Small ball tool

Small pieces of sponge

Instructions

1. Level top of cupcake, and spread buttercream evenly on top. Roll out 2½ ounces (70 grams) brown rolled fondant, and cut disc with round cutter. Lay disc on top of cupcake, and press gently to secure.

2. To make eye patch, roll a small ball of dark brown rolled fondant and flatten with your fingers. Affix to cupcake, just above center and to one side. To make muzzle, roll remaining brown rolled fondant into an oval, and flatten base. Cut an upside-down T-shape, and widen mouth with bone tool (**Figures A and B**). Affix muzzle to center of cupcake, and make indents for eyes using ball tool (**Figure C**).

3. To make ears, set aside a little dark brown rolled fondant for eyebrows, and roll the rest into two even sausage shapes. Flatten each sausage to form a teardrop shape (**Figure D**). Affix ears, and support with pieces of sponge until dry.

4. To make eyes, roll two small balls of black rolled fondant, and affix into indents. To make nose, roll remaining black rolled fondant into a triangle, and affix on muzzle, just above vertical cut. Roll red rolled fondant into a tongue shape, make a shallow cut down middle, and affix inside mouth (**Figure E**).

What a Wedding!

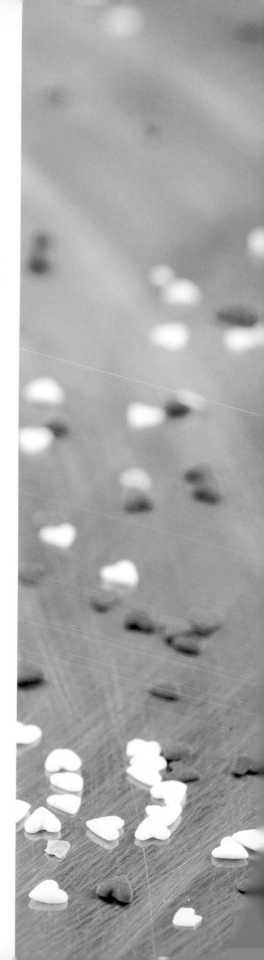

Celebrate in Silver

Materials

1 cupcake in silver baking cup

1 teaspoon (5 ml) buttercream or other spread

2½ ounces (70 grams) white rolled fondant

Silver dragées

White royal icing

Water

Tools

Serrated knife

Small spatula

Rolling pin

Large five-petal flower cutter

Medium heart cutter

Pastry bag and tip

Instructions

1. Level top of cupcake, and spread buttercream evenly on top. Roll out white rolled fondant, and cut flower and heart using flower and heart cutters (**Figure A**).

2. Affix flower onto cupcake, and press gently to secure. Affix heart onto center of flower and press gently to secure (**Figure B**).

3. Affix dragées around heart using royal icing (**Figure C**).

Heart-to-Heart

A

C

B

Materials

1 cupcake in heart-decorated baking cup

1 teaspoon (5 ml) buttercream or other spread

Rolled fondant in the following colors:

• 2½ ounces (70 grams) white

• ¾ ounce (21 grams) red

Plastic wrap

Tools

Serrated knife

Small spatula

Rolling pin

Small heart cutter

Plastic wrap

3-inch (7.5 cm) fluted round cutter

Instructions

1. Level top of cupcake, and spread buttercream evenly on top. Roll out white rolled fondant and cover with plastic wrap.

2. Roll out red rolled fondant and cut 20 hearts using heart cutter. Remove plastic wrap from white rolled fondant and place hearts on top so that they are evenly spaced and positioned in various directions (**Figure A**).

3. Cover with plastic wrap and roll gently to inlay. Remove plastic wrap and cut disc with fluted round cutter (**Figure B**).

4. Affix disc onto cupcake and press gently to secure (**Figure C**).

A

B

C

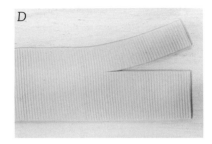

D

E

F

Materials

1 large cupcake in brown baking cup

2 teaspoons (10 ml) buttercream or other spread

Rolled fondant in the following colors:

- 10 ounces (283 grams) white
- 2 ounces (57 grams) light purple
- 5 ounces (142 grams) very light purple

Water

Light yellow royal icing

Tools

Serrated knife

Small spatula

Rolling pin

Pizza cutter

Thin lined rolling pin

Medium heart cutter

Pastry bag and tip

Instructions

1. Remove baking cup from cupcake, and level top. Spread buttercream evenly on top and sides (**Figure A**).

2. Roll out white rolled fondant and position on top of cupcake so that it hangs evenly all around. Press rolled fondant down around sides of cupcake, and trim along base with pizza cutter.

3. Using your thumb and pointer finger, pinch around top edge of cupcake to make a scalloped edge (**Figure B**).

4. Roll out light purple rolled fondant and re-roll once with lined rolling pin to make horizontal stripes. Cut out heart with heart cutter (**Figure C**).

5. Roll out very light purple rolled fondant into a strip long enough to fit around cupcake. Re-roll with lined rolling pin to make vertical stripes, and trim using pizza cutter (**Figure D**). Save scraps for sausage shape around base.

6. Affix lined strip around base of cupcake (**Figure E**).

7. Roll remaining very light purple rolled fondant into a sausage shape long enough to fit around cupcake, and affix around base. Pipe evenly spaced dots of royal icing along top of striped strip (**Figure F**).

Miniature Wedding Cake

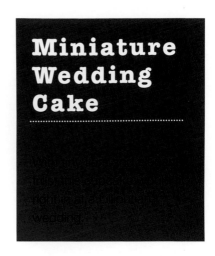

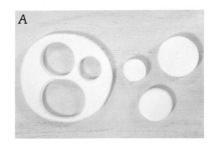

A

D

B

E

C

Materials

1 cupcake

1 teaspoon (5 ml) buttercream or other spread

Rolled fondant in the following colors:

• 2 ounces (57 grams) light pink

•1 ounce (28 grams) dark pink

• 2 ounces (57 grams) white

Water

White royal icing

Tools

Serrated knife

Small spatula

Rolling pin

3-inch (7.5 cm) plain round cutter

2¼-inch (5.7 cm) fluted round cutter

1¾-inch (4.5 cm) plain round cutter

1½-inch (3.8 cm) plain round cutter

1-inch (2.5 cm) plain round cutter

Pastry bag and tip

Instructions

1. Level top of cupcake, and spread buttercream evenly on top. Roll out light pink rolled fondant, and cut disc with largest plain round cutter. Lay disc on cupcake and press gently to secure.

2. Roll out dark pink rolled fondant. Cut disc with fluted round cutter and affix on cupcake.

3. Thickly roll out white rolled fondant (a width of about ½-inch (1.3 cm) is ideal) and cut three discs using the three smaller plain round cutters (Figure A).

4. Using your thumb and index finger, pinch around top edge of each disc to make scalloped edges (Figure B).

5. Affix discs in a mound, with largest disc on bottom (Figure C).

6. Affix tiered discs on cupcake (Figure D). Pipe evenly spaced dots of royal icing in a ring on top of each disc (Figure E).

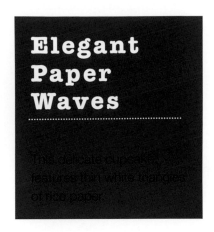

Elegant Paper Waves

This delicate cupcake features thin white triangles of rice paper.

Materials

1 cupcake

1 teaspoon (5 ml) buttercream or other spread

3¼ ounces (91 grams) white rolled fondant

Piece of white rice paper

Water

Tools

Serrated knife

Small spatula

Rolling pin

3-inch (7.5 cm) round cutter

Ruler

Sharp scissors

Pizza cutter

A

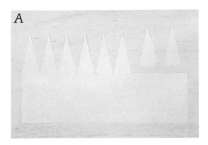

B

C

D

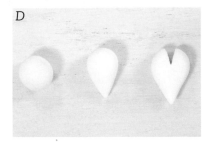

E

Instructions

1. Level top of cupcake, and spread buttercream evenly on top. Roll out 2½ ounces (70 grams) white rolled fondant, and cut disc with round cutter. Lay disc on cupcake and press gently to secure.

2. Cut rice paper into 16 triangles using template on page 119 (**Figure A**).

3. Apply a little water to shortest side of a rice paper triangle and affix at edge of cupcake. Apply water to another rice paper triangle, and affix so that it overlaps slightly with first triangle (**Figure B**). Repeat until all triangles are attached around top edge of cupcake.

4. Roll ½ ounce (14 grams) white rolled fondant into a thin strip long enough to fit around cupcake. Trim edges with pizza cutter, and affix around top of cupcake to conceal bottom edge of rice paper triangles (**Figure C**).

5. Shape remaining white rolled fondant into a teardrop shape. Cut out a wedge from rounded end to make heart shape (**Figure D**). Flatten heart with your fingers, and affix on cupcake (**Figure E**).

In the Garden

Dainty Daisy

Daisy, daisy, give me your answer do!

Materials

1 ounce (28 grams) white modeling paste

Rolled fondant in the following colors:

- ⅓ ounce (10 grams) yellow
- 2½ ounces (70 grams) light green
- 1 ounce (28 grams) dark green

1 cupcake

1 teaspoon (5 ml) buttercream or other spread

Water

Tools

Rolling pin

2½-inch (6.4 cm) daisy flower cutter

Toothpick

Aluminum foil

Serrated knife

Small spatula

3-inch (7.5 cm) round cutter

Instructions

Six hours in advance

1. Thinly roll out white modeling paste, and cut flower using flower cutter. Roll each petal separately with toothpick so that petals widen and overlap (Figure A).

2. Roll aluminum foil into a thick 2-inch (5 cm) ring. (Diameter of ring must be smaller than diameter of flower, but larger than diameter of flower center.) Position flower on ring so that center of flower lies over center of ring. Press down flower center so that petals are pushed upward, and use toothpick to lift every second petal, so that they rest on adjacent petals. To make flower center, roll yellow rolled fondant into a ball and flatten slightly. Set flower and center aside to dry for 6 hours (Figure B).

Assembling cupcake

3. Level top of cupcake, and spread buttercream evenly on top. Roll out light green rolled fondant, and cut disc with round cutter. Lay disc on cupcake and press gently to secure.

4. Roll dark green rolled fondant into a sausage shape long enough to fit around cupcake (Figure C), and affix (Figure D).

5. When flower is dry, remove from support ring. Affix flower center (Figure E), and affix flower to cupcake (Figure F).

Private Garden

This garden is bright and lovely . . . and never needs watering!

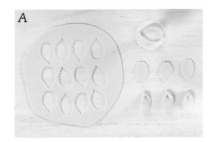

A

C

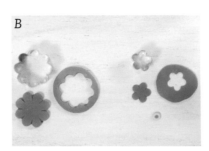

B

D

Materials

1 ounce (28 grams) light green modeling paste

Rolled fondant in the following colors:

- ¼ ounce (7 grams) pink
- ⅛ ounce (4 grams) orange
- Tiny amount yellow
- 2½ ounces (70 grams) dark green

Water

1 cupcake

1 teaspoon (5 ml) buttercream or other spread

Tools

Rolling pin

Small leaf cutter

1¾-inch (4.5 cm) flower cutter

¾-inch (1.9 cm) flower cutter

2-inch (5 cm) green floral wire

Serrated knife

Small spatula

3-inch (7.5 cm) round cutter

Instructions

Six hours in advance

1. Very thinly roll out light green modeling paste, and cut 15 leaves using leaf cutter. (This quantity allows for a few spares, in case any break during assembly.) Pinch bottom of each leaf, and set aside to dry for 6 hours (Figure A).

2. Thickly roll out pink rolled fondant, and cut flower using larger flower cutter. Thinly roll out orange rolled fondant, and cut flower using smaller flower cutter (Figure B).

3. Insert floral wire into pink flower so that it extends like a stem from bottom of flower. Take care that wire does not poke out in front or back of flower. Affix orange flower to center of pink flower. Roll a small ball of yellow rolled fondant and a smaller ball of orange fondant. Affix orange ball to center of yellow ball, and affix yellow ball to center of orange flower. Set aside to dry for 6 hours.

Assembling cupcake

4. Level top of cupcake, and spread buttercream evenly on top. Roll out dark green rolled fondant, and cut disc with round cutter. Lay disc on cupcake and press gently to secure.

5. Insert leaves in a ring around edge of cupcake (Figure C).

6. Insert flower stem into center of cupcake (Figure D).

Make sure wire stem is removed before cupcake is eaten!

Freshly Picked Flower

This design is simple and fun. A great project for young cupcake designers.

Materials

1 cupcake

1 teaspoon (5 ml) buttercream or other spread

Rolled fondant in the following colors:

- 2½ ounces (70 grams) dark green
- 3 ounces (85 grams) yellow
- ⅓ ounce (10 grams) purple

Water

Tools

Serrated knife

Small spatula

Rolling pin

3-inch (7.5 cm) fluted round cutter

Bone tool

A

B

C

D

Instructions

1. Level top of cupcake, and spread buttercream evenly on top. Roll out dark green rolled fondant, and cut disc with fluted round cutter. Lay disc on cupcake and press gently to secure. Make indents around edge of cupcake using bone tool (Figure A).

2. Shape yellow rolled fondant into six even teardrop shapes. Roll purple rolled fondant into a ball (Figure B).

3. Orient petals so that pointed ends meet in center of cupcake (Figure C).

4. Affix purple ball in center of flower (Figure D).

Field of Flowers

This design resembles a field of blooming wildflowers.

A

C

B

D

Materials

Rolled fondant in the following colors:

- 2½ ounces (70 grams) light green
- 1½ ounces (42 grams) red
- ⅓ ounce (10 grams) orange
- ⅓ ounce (10 grams) dark green

1 cupcake

1 teaspoon (5 ml) buttercream or other spread

Tools

Rolling pin

Plastic wrap

Small flower cutter

3-inch (7.5 cm) fluted round cutter

Serrated knife

Small spatula

Instructions

1. Thickly roll out light green rolled fondant and cover with plastic wrap. Thinly roll out red rolled fondant and cover with plastic wrap. Keep both sheets of rolled fondant covered as much as possible during next step to prevent them from drying out.

2. Cut flowers of red rolled fondant using small flower cutter (Figure A). Roll small balls of orange rolled fondant for flower centers. Shape tiny teardrop shapes of dark green rolled fondant for leaves. Arrange flowers, flower centers, and leaves on light green rolled fondant (Figure B).

3. Cover decorated rolled fondant with plastic wrap and roll gently to inlay. Remove plastic wrap and cut disc with fluted round cutter (Figure C).

4. Level top of cupcake, and spread buttercream evenly on top. Affix disc onto cupcake and press gently to secure (Figure D).

Springtime Blossoms

Celebrate the first day of spring (or any other day!) with this flowery tree. Be sure to remove skewer before serving.

A

D

B

E

C

Materials

1 ounce (28 grams) green modeling paste

Rolled fondant in the following colors:

- ⅓ ounce (10 grams) orange
- Tiny amount red
- 2½ ounces (70 grams) light brown
- 3 ounces (85 grams) dark brown

Water

1 cupcake

1 teaspoon (5 ml) buttercream or other spread

Tools

Rolling pin

Small flower cutter

Wooden skewers

Serrated knife

Small spatula

3-inch (7.5 cm) plain round cutter

Bone tool

Small sharp knife

Instructions

Six hours in advance

1. To make treetop, thickly roll out green modeling paste and cut using template on page 119. Thinly roll out orange rolled fondant and cut several flowers using flower cutter (Figure A). Roll tiny balls of red rolled fondant and affix to center of each flower. Affix flowers to treetop and insert skewer into bottom of treetop, pressing it up until it almost reaches top (taking care that it doesn't poke through). Set aside to dry for 6 hours (Figure B).

Assembling cupcake

2. Level top of cupcake, and spread buttercream evenly on top. Roll out light brown rolled fondant, and cut disc with round cutter. Lay disc on cupcake and press gently to secure.

3. Shape tree trunk with branches and roots using dark brown rolled fondant. Make creases and indents using bone tool and knife. Draw a skewer through trunk so that it makes a hole from top to bottom of trunk (Figure C).

4. Place trunk on center of cupcake, arranging roots so that trunk is stable (Figure D).

5. Insert skewer extending from treetop into trunk, and affix branches (Figure E).

Make sure wooden skewer is removed before cupcake is eaten!

A Multitude of Monsters

Blue Monster

You'll never be blue with a happy monster like this by your side.

A

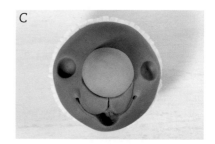

C

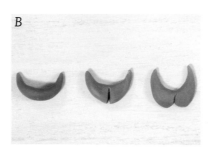

B

D

Materials

1 cupcake

1 teaspoon (5 ml) buttercream or other spread

Rolled fondant in the following colors:

- 2½ ounces (70 grams) blue
- ¾ ounce (21 grams) purple
- ⅓ ounce (10 grams) red
- Small amount white
- ¹⁄₁₀ ounce (3 grams) yellow
- Tiny amount black
- Small amount orange

Water

Tools

Serrated knife

Small spatula

Rolling pin

3-inch (7.5 cm) round cutter

Large and small ball tools

Small sharp knife

Bone tool

Pieces of dry spaghetti

Toothpick

Instructions

1. Level top of cupcake, and spread buttercream evenly on top. Roll out blue rolled fondant, and cut disc with round cutter. Set aside scraps for upper lip. Lay disc on cupcake and press gently to secure. Make indents for eyes with large ball tool (Figure A).

2. To make lip, roll remaining blue rolled fondant into a thick crescent and flatten. Make a vertical cut in middle of crescent; then shape a rounded flap on either side of cut (Figure B).

3. To make nose, roll purple rolled fondant into a ball, flatten base, and affix in center of cupcake. Affix lip just below nose. Cut moon-shaped mouth and widen with bone tool (Figure C).

4. To make horns, shape red rolled fondant into two even teardrop shapes. Bend pointed end of each teardrop shape, and partially insert a piece of spaghetti into base of each horn. Orient horns so pointed ends face outward, and insert exposed spaghetti into cupcake.

5. To make teeth, roll out white rolled fondant and affix inside mouth. Cut one horizontal line and several vertical lines. To make eyes, roll yellow rolled fondant into two even balls. Affix balls in indents, and indent each eye with small ball tool. Roll two tiny balls of black rolled fondant and affix onto eyes. Mark center of each eye with toothpick.

6. To make hair, shape orange rolled fondant into three even teardrop shapes. Orient teardrop shapes so that pointed ends join, and affix (Figure D).

Make sure pieces of dry spaghetti are removed before cupcake is eaten!

Green Monster

Others will be green with envy when they see this happy monster!

A

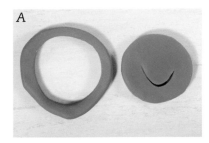

D

B

C

E

Materials

1 cupcake

1 teaspoon (5 ml) buttercream or other spread

Rolled fondant in the following colors:

- 2½ ounces (70 grams) dark green
- Small amount white
- ⅛ ounce (4 grams) yellow
- ¹⁄₁₀ ounce (3 grams) red
- Tiny amount orange
- ⅓ ounce (10 grams) blue
- 1 ounce (28 grams) light green

Water

Tools

Serrated knife

Small spatula

Rolling pin

3-inch (7.5 cm) round cutter

Small sharp knife

Toothpick

Large and small ball tools

Pieces of dry spaghetti

Instructions

1. Level top of cupcake, and spread buttercream evenly on top. Roll out dark green rolled fondant, and cut disc with round cutter. Cut moon-shaped mouth (Figure A). Lay disc on cupcake and press gently to secure.

2. Widen mouth and shape lips with your fingers. Lift top lip and use toothpick to draw up ends and form cheeks. Make indents for eyes using large ball tool (Figure B).

3. To make teeth, roll white rolled fondant into a crescent shape and affix inside mouth. To make eyes, roll yellow rolled fondant into two even balls. Affix balls in indents, and indent each eye with small ball tool. To make nose, shape red rolled fondant into a teardrop shape and affix (Figure C). Roll orange rolled fondant into two even balls, and affix onto eyes. Mark center of each eye with toothpick.

4. To make eyebrows, shape two small teardrop shapes of blue rolled fondant. Affix over eyes so that thicker parts meet. To make hair, shape remaining blue rolled fondant into three larger teardrop shapes and two smaller teardrop shapes. Flatten teardrop bottoms and affix.

5. To make arms, shape light green rolled fondant into two even sausage shapes. Flatten one end of each sausage shape, and shape other end into a ball. Flatten ball gently, and cut out fingers and a thumb. Partially insert a piece of spaghetti into flat end of each arm (Figure D). Insert exposed spaghetti into cupcake (Figure E).

Make sure pieces of dry spaghetti are removed before cupcake is eaten!

Purple Monster

This purple monster is positively preposterous!

Materials

1 cupcake

1 teaspoon (5 ml) buttercream or other spread

Rolled fondant in the following colors:
- 2½ ounces (70 grams) purple
- Small amount red
- ¹⁄₁₀ ounce (3 grams) orange
- ⅓ ounce (10 grams) yellow
- Tiny amount white
- Small amount light purple
- Small amount light blue
- Tiny amount green

Water

Tools

Serrated knife

Small spatula

Rolling pin

3-inch (7.5 cm) round cutter

Small sharp knife

Toothpick

Bone tool

Pieces of dry spaghetti

Small ball tool

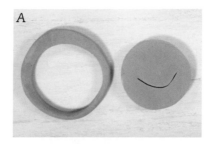

A

B

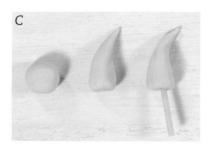

C

D

Instructions

1. Level top of cupcake, and spread buttercream evenly on top. Roll out purple rolled fondant, and cut disc with round cutter. Set aside scraps for ears. Cut moon-shaped mouth (Figure A). Lay disc on cupcake, model a chin, and press gently to secure.

2. Widen mouth and shape lips with your fingers. Lift top lip and use toothpick to draw up ends into cheeks. Make oval indents for eyes with bone tool.

3. To make lips, roll red rolled fondant into a crescent shape, and affix inside mouth. Make shallow cut to separate top and bottom lips. To make nose, shape orange rolled fondant into a teardrop shape and affix (Figure B).

4. To make horns, shape yellow rolled fondant into two even cones. Curve horns gently; then partially insert a piece of spaghetti into base of each horn (Figure C). Orient horns so pointed ends face inward; then insert exposed spaghetti into cupcake.

5. To make teeth, roll out white rolled fondant and cut into a small square. Make a partial cut down middle of square, separate bottom of teeth slightly, and affix inside mouth. To make ears, shape remaining purple rolled fondant into two even balls, and flatten balls on one side. Shape light purple rolled fondant into two even balls, and flatten on one side. Affix light purple balls onto purple balls, indent with bone tool, and affix on cupcake.

6. To make eyes, shape blue rolled fondant into even ovals. Affix in indents, and indent each eye with ball tool. Roll green rolled fondant into two even balls, and affix onto eyes. Mark center of each eye with toothpick (Figure D).

Make sure pieces of dry spaghetti are removed before cupcake is eaten!

Pink Monster

Even people who don't generally like monsters will be tickled pink by this friendly fiend.

Materials

⅒ ounce (3 grams) yellow modeling paste

1 cupcake

1 teaspoon (5 ml) buttercream or other spread

Rolled fondant in the following colors:

- ⅙ ounce (5 grams) red
- 3 ounces (85 grams) pink
- ⅙ ounce (5 grams) white
- Small amount green
- Tiny amount purple

Tools

Piece of dry spaghetti

Serrated knife

Small spatula

Rolling pin

Small sharp knife

3-inch (7.5 cm) round cutter

Small ball tool

Bone tool

Toothpick

Instructions

Two hours in advance

1. To make hair, roll yellow modeling paste into a thin sausage shape. Wrap several times around a piece of spaghetti, and set aside to dry for 2 hours (Figure A).

A

B

C

D

E

F

Assembling cupcake

2. Level top of cupcake, and spread buttercream evenly on top. Thinly roll out red rolled fondant, and cut into a rectangle wide enough to cover most of cupcake. Position rectangle on cupcake in mouth area, and press gently to secure (Figure B).

3. Roll out 2½ ounces (70 grams) pink rolled fondant, and cut disc with round cutter. Set aside scraps for ears. Cut out moon-shaped mouth (Figure C). Lay disc on cupcake, taking care that red rolled fondant is visible through mouth. (Open area on pink rolled fondant will widen as fondant is affixed onto cupcake, so make sure only red is visible.) Press gently to secure.

4. Make indents for eyes using ball tool. Make indents for ears using bone tool (Figure D). Make a small indent at top of cupcake for affixing hair.

5. Thinly roll out white rolled fondant, cut teeth using template on page 120, and affix.

6. To make eyes, roll purple rolled fondant into two even balls. Affix in indents; then mark center of each eye with toothpick. To make nose, roll green rolled fondant into an oval, and affix.

7. To make ears, shape remaining pink rolled fondant into two even, elongated teardrop shapes. Partially insert a piece of spaghetti into narrow end of each ear (Figure E). Insert exposed end of spaghetti into indents.

8. When hair is dry, remove carefully from spaghetti and affix at top of cupcake (Figure F).

Make sure pieces of dry spaghetti are removed before cupcake is eaten!

Orange Monster

This cheeky monster is bright, beautiful, and full of character!

A

B

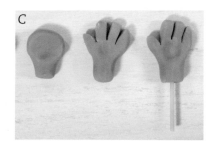

C

D

Materials

1 cupcake

1 teaspoon (5 ml) buttercream or other spread

Rolled fondant in the following colors:

- 3 ounces (85 grams) orange
- Small amount yellow
- Tiny amount blue
- Tiny amount green
- ⅔ ounce (19 grams) purple

Modeling paste in the following color:

- Tiny amount red

Water

Tools

Serrated knife

Small spatula

Rolling pin

3-inch (7.5 cm) round cutter

Small sharp knife

Small and medium ball tools

Bone tool

Toothpick

Pieces of dry spaghetti

Instructions

1. Level top of cupcake, and spread buttercream evenly on top. Roll two small balls of orange rolled fondant and position on cupcake in cheek area (Figure A).

2. Roll out remaining orange rolled fondant, and cut disc with round cutter. Set aside scraps for ears. Lay disc on cupcake, carefully arranging balls so they are in just the right place, and press gently to secure. Cut small U-shaped mouth, and indent middle with small ball tool. Indent eyes with medium ball tool (Figure B).

3. To make nose, divide yellow rolled fondant in half and shape one half into an oval. Flatten base, affix on cupcake, and indent nostrils with bone tool. To make ears, shape remaining orange rolled fondant into two even cones. Shape remaining yellow rolled fondant into two even cones. Affix yellow cones on orange cones, indent with bone tool, and affix on cupcake.

4. To make eyes, shape green rolled fondant into two even balls. Affix in indents, and indent each eye with toothpick. To make eyebrows, shape blue rolled fondant into two even teardrop shapes. Affix above eyes, with thickest part of teardrops facing inward. To make lips, roll some red modeling paste into a tiny ball, press into mouth, and shape with bone tool. Roll remaining red rolled fondant into a thin sausage shape, twist into a curl, and affix at top of cupcake for hair.

5. To make hands, shape light purple rolled fondant into two even balls. Flatten top of balls and cut out fingers and a thumb. Shape base into a cylinder. Partially insert a piece of spaghetti into base of each hand (Figure C). Insert exposed spaghetti into cupcake (Figure D).

Make sure pieces of dry spaghetti are removed before cupcake is eaten!

Yellow Monster

With a goofy nose and multi-colored eyes, this monster will draw more giggles than gasps.

Materials

¹⁄₁₀ ounce (3 grams) black modeling paste

1 cupcake

1 teaspoon (5 ml) buttercream or other spread

Rolled fondant in the following colors:

- 2½ ounces (70 grams) yellow
- Small amount orange
- Tiny amount blue
- ¹⁄₁₀ ounce (3 grams) purple
- Tiny amount green
- ¾ ounce (21 grams) red

Water

Tools

Small sharp knife

Serrated knife

Small spatula

Rolling pin

3-inch (7.5 cm) round cutter

Toothpick

Wooden skewer

Large, medium, and small ball tools

A

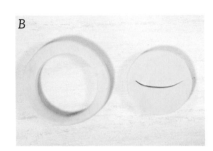

B

C

D

Instructions

One hour in advance

1. To make hair, roll black modeling paste into a long thin cylinder. Cut cylinder into five uneven pieces and set aside for 1 hour to dry (Figure A).

Assembling cupcake

2. Level top of cupcake, and spread buttercream evenly on top. Roll out yellow rolled fondant, and cut disc with round cutter. Set aside scraps for ears. Cut wide, moon-shaped mouth (Figure B). Lay disc on cupcake and press gently to secure.

3. Use toothpick to deepen mouth and draw up ends to form cheeks. Make indents for eyes using large ball tool (Figure C). Make five indents for hair along top of cupcake using skewer. (Check to make sure hair fits inside indents.)

4. To make ears, shape two even cones of yellow rolled fondant. Shape two even balls of orange rolled fondant, and affix onto yellow cones. Indent ears with bone tool and affix on cupcake.

5. To make eyes, shape purple rolled fondant into two even balls. Affix on cupcake and indent each eye with medium ball tool. Shape two even balls of blue rolled fondant and affix inside purple balls. Indent blue parts of eyes with small ball tool. Shape two even balls of green rolled fondant and affix inside blue balls. Mark center of each eye with toothpick.

6. To make nose, shape red rolled fondant into a teardrop shape and affix. When hair is completely dry, affix into holes (Figure D)

The Wild Ones

Mischievous Monkey

Monkey see, monkey do, monkey eat!

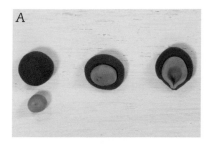

A

C

B

D

Materials

1 cupcake

1 teaspoon (5 ml) buttercream or other spread

Rolled fondant in the following colors:
- 2½ ounces (70 grams) dark brown
- 2 ounces (57 grams) light brown
- Tiny amount red
- Tiny amount black
- Tiny amount white

Water

Tools

Serrated knife

Small spatula

Rolling pin

3-inch (7.5 cm) round cutter

Small ball tool

Bone tool

Small sharp knife

Instructions

1. Level top of cupcake, and spread buttercream evenly on top. Roll out dark brown rolled fondant, and cut disc with round cutter. Set aside scraps for ears and hair. Lay disc on cupcake and press gently to secure. Make one indent on top of cupcake and two indents on either side for ears.

2. Divide remaining dark brown rolled fondant into three even pieces. Use one piece to make ears by shaping it into two even ovals. Roll two smaller ovals of light brown rolled fondant, and affix onto larger ovals. Indent with bone tool and pinch at one end (Figure A). Affix on cupcake.

3. Use another piece of dark brown rolled fondant to make hair by shaping four even teardrop shapes. Orient teardrops so that pointed ends join, and affix. Gently press into indent at top of cupcake.

4. To make eyes, roll out a little light brown rolled fondant and cut using template on page 120. Affix just above center of cupcake, and indent eyes with ball tool (Figure B).

5. To make muzzle, set aside a little light brown rolled fondant for eyebrows, and roll the rest into a ball. Flatten base and cut mouth near bottom. Widen and shape mouth with your fingers, and cut a line from top of muzzle to mouth. To make nose, shape remaining piece of dark brown rolled fondant into a rounded triangle. Indent nostrils with ball tool and affix on muzzle (Figure C).

6. Affix muzzle on cupcake. Roll red rolled fondant into a small ball, affix inside mouth, and shape with bone tool. To make eyes, roll two even balls of white rolled fondant and affix. Roll two even balls of black rolled fondant and affix onto white balls. To make eyebrows, shape remaining light brown rolled fondant into two tiny teardrop shapes, blend slightly, and affix (Figure D).

Lovable Lion

This character isn't just king of the jungle. He is king of the cupcakes, too.

Materials

1 cupcake

1 teaspoon (5 ml) buttercream or other spread

Rolled fondant in the following colors:

- 4 ounces (114 grams) light brown
- 2 ounces (57 grams) dark brown
- Tiny amount white
- 1/10 ounce (3 grams) black

Water

Tools

Serrated knife

Small spatula

Rolling pin

3-inch (7.5 cm) round cutter

Small sharp knife

Bone tool

Small and medium ball tools

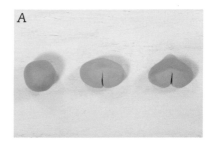

A

B

C

D

Instructions

1. Level top of cupcake, and spread buttercream evenly on top. Roll out 2½ ounces (70 grams) light brown rolled fondant, and cut disc with round cutter. Lay disc on top of cupcake and press gently to secure.

2. To make muzzle, roll ⅔ ounce (21 grams) light brown rolled fondant into a rounded triangle. Make a vertical cut in middle of base, and shape cheeks on either side of cut (Figure A).

3. Affix muzzle to cupcake, and smooth down top (Figure B).

4. Divide remaining light brown rolled fondant into three even pieces. To make ears, shape two pieces into teardrop shapes. Indent with bone tool and affix on cupcake. To make mouth, shape third piece into a small pyramid and affix at bottom of muzzle. Make indents for eyes using medium ball tool.

5. To make mane, set aside a little dark brown rolled fondant for eyebrows, and shape the rest into twenty larger teardrop shapes and six smaller teardrop shapes. Bend tip of each teardrop shape and affix around edge of cupcake. Take care to affix smaller teardrop shapes in front of ears so as not to conceal them (Figure C).

6. To make eyes, shape white rolled fondant into two even balls. Affix on cupcake, and indent each eye with small ball tool. Shape two even balls of black rolled fondant and affix onto white balls. To make nose, roll remaining black rolled fondant into a rounded triangle and affix. To make eyebrows, shape two even teardrop shapes of dark brown rolled fondant and affix above eyes, with thickest part of teardrop shapes facing inward (Figure D).

Very Happy Hippo

You'll be hungrier than a hippo when you see this cupcake design.

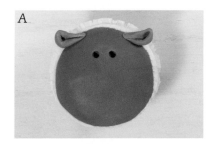

A

C

B

Materials

1 cupcake

1 teaspoon (5 ml) buttercream or other spread

Rolled fondant in the following colors:

• 5 ounces (142 grams) gray

• ⅙ ounce (5 grams) pink

• Tiny amount white

• Tiny amount black

Water

Tools

Serrated knife

Small spatula

Rolling pin

3-inch (7.5 cm) round cutter

Bone tool

Small sharp knife

Small ball tool

Instructions

1. Level top of cupcake, and spread buttercream evenly on top. Roll out 2½ ounces (70 grams) gray rolled fondant, and cut disc with round cutter. Lay disc on top of cupcake and press gently to secure.

2. To make ears, shape a little gray rolled fondant into two even teardrop shapes and indent with bone tool. Affix on either side of cupcake, near top. Make indents for eyes using ball tool (Figure A).

3. To make mouth, set aside a little gray rolled fondant for nostrils, and shape the rest into an oval. Flatten base, and cut moon-shaped mouth. Widen mouth using your fingers, and shape lips (Figure B).

4. Affix mouth on cupcake. To make nostrils, shape two even teardrop shapes of gray rolled fondant. (These should be smaller than the ears.) Indent using bone tool, and affix on mouth. To make tongue, thinly roll out pink rolled fondant. Trim into a tongue shape, affix into mouth, and mark a shallow cut down middle. To make teeth, roll two even cylinders of white rolled fondant and press into top of mouth.

5. To make eyes, roll two even balls of white rolled fondant and affix inside indents. Roll two even balls of black rolled fondant and affix onto eyes. To make eyebrows, shape two even teardrops of black rolled fondant and affix above eyes, with thickest part of teardrop shapes facing inward (Figure C).

A Tiger's Tale

There is nothing timid about this bright tiger. He is striped, bold, and very friendly.

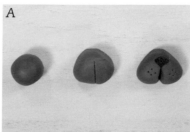

A

C

B

Materials

1 cupcake

1 teaspoon (5 ml) buttercream or other spread

Rolled fondant in the following colors:

- 4¼ ounces (121 grams) orange
- 2 ounces (57 grams) black
- Small amount white
- Tiny amount red

Water

Tools

Serrated knife

Small spatula

Rolling pin

3-inch (7.5 cm) round cutter

Small sharp knife

Toothpick

Small ball tool

Bone tool

Instructions

1. Level top of cupcake, and spread buttercream evenly on top. Roll out 2½ ounces (70 grams) orange rolled fondant, and cut disc with round cutter. Lay disc on cupcake and press gently to secure.

2. To make muzzle, roll 1½ ounces (42 grams) orange rolled fondant into a rounded triangle. Make a vertical cut in middle of base, and shape cheeks on either side of cut. Indent freckles with toothpick. To make nose, shape a small triangle of black rolled fondant and affix (Figure A).

3. Affix muzzle to cupcake. Make indents for eyes using ball tool. To make ears, shape two teardrop shapes of orange rolled fondant. Indent with bone tool and affix at top of cupcake. Set aside a little black rolled fondant for making eyes, and thinly roll out the rest. Cut seven small triangles; affix three at top of cupcake, and two on either side (Figure B).

4. To make eyes, roll two even balls of white rolled fondant and affix inside indents. Roll two even balls of black rolled fondant and affix onto white eyes. To make tongue, roll red rolled fondant into a small ball, indent with bone tool, and affix (Figure C).

Positively Panda

Though this design uses only two colors, it is brimming with personality.

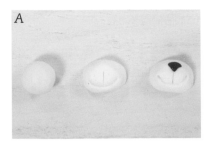

A

B

C

Materials

1 cupcake

1 teaspoon (5 ml) buttercream or other spread

Rolled fondant in the following colors:
- 4 ounces (114 grams) white
- 1 ounce (28 grams) black

Water

Tools

Serrated knife

Small spatula

Rolling pin

3-inch (7.5 cm) round cutter

Small sharp knife

Small ball tool

Instructions

1. Level top of cupcake, and spread buttercream evenly on top. Roll out 2½ ounces (70 grams) white rolled fondant, and cut disc with round cutter. Lay disc on top of cupcake and press gently to secure.

2. To make muzzle, roll 1 ounce (28 grams) white rolled fondant into an oval and flatten base. Cut narrow moon-shaped mouth, and make a vertical cut upward. To make nose, shape a small triangle of black rolled fondant and affix (Figure A).

3. Affix muzzle on cupcake. Roll out a little black rolled fondant and cut two eye patches using template on page 120. Affix patches on an angle just above muzzle. Make indents for eyes and ears with ball tool (Figure B).

4. To make ears, shape two small teardrop shapes of black rolled fondant, indent with bone tool, and affix on either side of cupcake. To make eyes, roll two even balls of white rolled fondant and affix in indents. Roll two even balls of black rolled fondant and affix onto eyes. To make eyebrows, roll two tiny teardrop shapes of black rolled fondant and affix (Figure C).

Celebrating Baby

Cute as a Bunny

With extended arms and friendly floppy ears, this bunny seems to say "Hug me!"

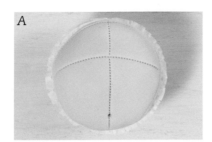

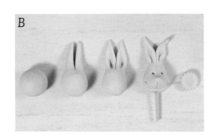

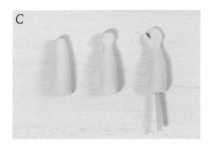

Materials

1 cupcake

1 teaspoon (5 ml) buttercream or other spread

Rolled fondant in the following colors:

• 4 ounces (114 grams) light blue

• Tiny amount pink

• Tiny amount turquoise

Water

White royal icing (optional)

Tools

Serrated knife

Small spatula

Rolling pin

3-inch (7.5 cm) round cutter

Design wheeler

Small ball tool

Pieces of dry spaghetti

Bone tool

Small sharp knife

Toothpick

Light blue ribbon

Decorating bag and tip (optional)

Instructions

1. Level top of cupcake, and spread buttercream evenly on top. Roll out 2½ ounces (70 grams) light blue rolled fondant. Cut disc with round cutter. Lay disc on cupcake and press gently to secure. Use design wheeler to mark one vertical and one horizontal line on cupcake, so that lines intersect ⅔ of the way between center and back of cupcake. Mark another seam around circumference of cupcake, close to edge. Mark belly button with ball tool near front of cupcake (Figure A).

2. To make head, shape ¾ ounce (21 grams) light blue rolled fondant into a teardrop. Make a cut down middle of narrow end to separate ears. Shape ears into teardrop shapes, and indent front of each ear with bone tool. Make indents for eyes using ball tool. Cut crescent-shaped mouth and make a vertical cut to nose. Partially insert a piece of spaghetti into bottom of head. To make neck, roll a small ball of light blue rolled fondant and flatten. Cut vertical lines all around edge (Figure B).

3. Affix neck to cupcake where seamed lines intersect. Insert exposed spaghetti through center of neck, and into cupcake. Mark a seam down middle of head with design wheeler. To make eyes, roll turquoise rolled fondant into two even balls and affix. Indent middle of each eye with toothpick. To make nose, shape pink rolled fondant into a rounded triangle and affix.

4. To make arms, roll remaining light blue rolled fondant into two even sausage shapes. Flatten one end of each sausage shape to make base, and shape other end into a ball. Flatten balls gently, and make a cut to separate thumb. Partially insert a piece of dry spaghetti into base of each arm (Figure C). Insert exposed spaghetti into cupcake. When arms are securely in place, mark seams along arm and around wrist with design wheeler.

5. Tie ribbon in a bow and affix on cupcake just below neck (Figure D). (To affix ribbon, you can moisten rolled fondant with a bit of water or use a drop of royal icing.)

Make sure pieces of dry spaghetti are removed before cupcake is eaten!

Pacifier, Please

Don't be surprised if children at your party prefer this pacifier to their own!

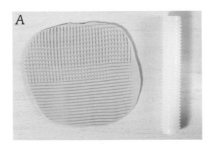

A

C

B

D

Materials

1 cupcake

1 teaspoon (5 ml) buttercream or other spread

Rolled fondant in the following colors:

- 2½ ounces (70 grams) light green
- 2½ ounces (70 grams) white
- ⅔ ounce (21 grams) brown
- ⅓ ounce (10 grams) light blue

Water

Tools

Serrated knife

Small spatula

Rolling pin

3-inch (7.5 cm) round cutter

Thick lined rolling pin

Pizza cutter

1½-inch (3.8 cm) round cutter

Pieces of sponge

Instructions

1. Level top of cupcake, and spread buttercream evenly on top. Roll out white rolled fondant, and cut disc with larger round cutter. Lay disc on top of cupcake and press gently to secure.

2. To make blanket, thinly roll out light green rolled fondant to an area that is about 5 × 5 inches (12.7 × 12.7 cm). Re-roll once vertically then horizontally using lined rolling pin to make a crisscross pattern (Figure A). Trim edges and fold gently onto cupcake.

3. To make pacifier, roll ½ ounce (14 grams) brown rolled fondant into a cylinder. Round cylinder at one end, and taper other end into nipple shape (Figure B).

4. Roll remaining brown rolled fondant into a thin sausage shape. Bend into a horseshoe shape, then turn in ends to form handle. Roll out light blue rolled fondant, and cut disc with smaller round cutter (Figure C).

5. Connect pacifier parts, and support handle with pieces of sponge until dry. Affix pacifier onto cupcake (Figure D).

Baby Booty

Many people cherish baby's first booties.

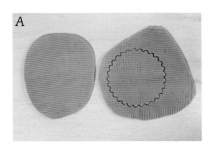

A

B

C

Materials

1 cupcake

1 teaspoon (5 ml) buttercream or other spread

Rolled fondant in the following colors:

• 2½ ounces (70 grams) light purple

• 2 ounces (57 grams) white

Water

White royal icing

Tools

Serrated knife

Small spatula

Rolling pin

Thin lined rolling pin

3-inch (7.5 cm) fluted round cutter

Design wheeler

Pink ribbon

Pastry bag and tip

Instructions

1. Level top of cupcake, and spread buttercream evenly on top. Roll out light purple rolled fondant. Re-roll once vertically then horizontally using lined rolling pin to make a crisscross pattern. Cut disc with fluted round cutter (Figure A). Lay disc on top of cupcake and press gently to secure.

2. To make bootie, roll white rolled fondant into a ball; then shape by drawing cuff area upward and toe areas forward. Indent top of cuff, and mark seam around sole using design wheeler (Figure B).

3. Pipe dots of royal icing around top of cuff, and along top of foot. Pipe a heart in middle of foot. Tie ribbon in a bow and affix using royal icing. Affix bootie on cupcake (Figure C).

Bear on Bib

Here is a bib that even the fussiest baby will love to wear.

A

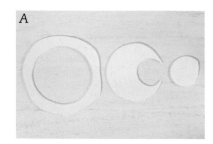

C

B

D

Materials

1 cupcake

1 teaspoon (5 ml) buttercream or other spread

Rolled fondant in the following colors:

• 2½ ounces (70 grams) white

• 1 ounce (28 grams) light blue

• Tiny amount light yellow

• Small amount light orange

Water

White royal icing (optional)

Tools

Serrated knife

Small spatula

Rolling pin

3-inch (7.5 cm) round cutter

2½-inch (6.4 cm) round cutter

1½-inch (3.8 cm) round cutter

Toothpick

Design wheeler

Small bear cutter

Light pink ribbon

Decorating bag and tip (optional)

Instructions

1. Level top of cupcake, and spread buttercream evenly on top. Roll out white rolled fondant, and cut disc with largest round cutter. Lay disc on top of cupcake and press gently to secure.

2. To make bib, thinly roll out light blue rolled fondant, and cut disc with medium round cutter. Cut disc into a crescent shape by removing a section with smallest round cutter (Figure A).

3. Roll toothpick around outer edge of bib to frill. Use design wheeler to mark seam along inner edge of frill and inside of collar. To make buttons, roll two tiny balls of light yellow rolled fondant, and then flatten. Mark four holes on each button using toothpick (Figure B).

4. To make bear, roll out light yellow rolled fondant and cut with bear cutter. Use scraps to shape a small round nose and affix. Use toothpick to indent eyes and belly button (Figure C).

5. Affix bib to cupcake, laying base flat but allowing edge to frill. Affix bear in middle of bib, and affix buttons. Tie ribbon into a bow, and affix edges of ribbon to edges of bib (Figure D). (To affix ribbon, moisten rolled fondant with a bit of water, or use a drop of royal icing.)

Baby Face

It's a boy! It's a girl! It's an adorable cupcake!

A

C

B

D

Materials

1 cupcake

1 teaspoon (5 ml) buttercream or other spread

Rolled fondant in the following colors:

- 2½ ounces (70 grams) flesh-colored
- Tiny amount orange
- Tiny amount pink
- Tiny amount light blue
- 1 ounce (28 grams) light purple
- Tiny amount yellow

Water

Brown food coloring marker

Tools

Serrated knife

Small spatula

Rolling pin

3-inch (7.5 cm) plain round cutter

Bone tool

Small ball tool

3-inch (7.5 cm) fluted round cutter

Instructions

1. Level top of cupcake, and spread buttercream evenly on top. Roll out flesh-colored rolled fondant, and cut disc with plain round cutter. Save scraps for nose and ears. Lay disc on top of cupcake, pressing gently to secure.

2. Divide leftover flesh-colored rolled fondant into three even pieces. To make nose, roll one piece into an oval and affix. Roll two other pieces into ovals, shape into ears using bone tool, and affix. Make indents for eyes using ball tool (Figure A).

3. To make pacifier, roll a small ball of orange rolled fondant, flatten gently with your fingers, and affix below nose. Roll a smaller ball of pink rolled fondant, flatten, and affix on orange ball. To make eyes, roll two tiny balls of light blue rolled fondant and affix into indents (Figure B).

4. To make bonnet, thickly roll out light purple rolled fondant and cut disc with fluted round cutter. Cut disc into a crescent shape by removing a section with plain round cutter (Figure C). Affix bonnet around top of head.

5. To make hair, roll yellow rolled fondant into a thin sausage shape and coil. Affix in middle of forehead. Draw eyebrows with brown food coloring pen (Figure D).

Teddy Bear

This bear looks cute enough to cuddle (and is sweet enough to eat!)

Materials

1 cupcake

1 teaspoon (5 ml) buttercream or other spread

Rolled fondant in the following colors:

• 3½ ounces (100 grams) white

• 2 ounces (57 grams) pink

• Tiny amount orange

• Tiny amount light blue

Water

Tools

Serrated knife

Small spatula

Rolling pin

Thick lined rolling pin

3-inch (7.5 cm) fluted round cutter

Small sharp knife

Design wheeler

Toothpick

Bone tool

Drinking straw, cut in half lengthwise

A

B

C

D

Instructions

1. Level top of cupcake, and spread buttercream evenly on top. Roll out 2½ ounces (70 grams) white rolled fondant. Re-roll once vertically then horizontally using lined rolling pin to make a crisscross pattern (Figure A). Cut disc with fluted round cutter. Lay disc on top of cupcake and press gently to secure.

2. To make pillow, shape remaining white rolled fondant into a thick rectangle. Pinch corners and add creases (Figure B). Affix near top of cupcake.

3. To make bear, divide pink rolled fondant into three even pieces. To make body, shape one piece into a teardrop shape, and flatten base. Flatten four areas on sides to affix arms and legs. Mark seam down middle with design wheeler, and indent belly button with toothpick.

4. Use second piece of pink rolled fondant to make head. Set aside a little for ears and muzzle. Shape the rest into a ball and mark eyes with toothpick. Shape two round ears, indent with bone tool, and affix. Shape a small ball and flatten, for muzzle. Press in halved drinking straw to indent mouth, and make a short vertical cut to nose. Roll a tiny ball of orange rolled fondant for nose.

5. To make arms and legs, divide third piece into two smaller and two larger pieces. Shape all four pieces into sausage shapes that are wider at one end. Shape narrower ends into balls, and flatten to make feet and hands. Shape wider ends so that they can be affixed onto body (Figure C).

6. Affix body to cupcake surface, so that top of body is adjacent to pillow. Affix head so that it leans on pillow, and affix arms and legs. Roll tiny balls of light blue rolled fondant for eyes, and then affix (Figure D).

Happy Birthday

Say It with Cupcakes!

This is a great design for saying what you really mean. Plan your message in advance, so that you can select colors and trim plaques to size.

A

C

B

Materials

Rolled fondant in the following colors:

- 3 ounces (85 grams) various pastel colors
- 2½ ounces (70 grams) orange
- 2½ ounces (70 grams) yellow
- 2½ ounces (70 grams) green

2 ounces (57 grams) black modeling paste

Water

3 cupcakes

3 teaspoons (15 ml) buttercream or other spread

Tools

Rolling pin

Alphabet cutters

Small sharp knife

Serrated knife

Small spatula

3-inch (7.5 cm) round cutter

Instructions

Six hours in advance

1. Write out your message and decide on letter colors. Roll out selected rolled fondant colors, and cut letters using alphabet cutters.

2. Arrange letters on work surface, and trim places where letters overlap (Figure A).

3. Thickly roll out black modeling paste, and cut plaques using templates on pages 121–123. Trim templates to fit word length, if necessary (Figure B).

4. Affix letters on plaques and set aside to dry for 6 hours.

Assembling cupcakes

5. Level tops of cupcakes, and spread buttercream evenly on top. Roll out orange, yellow, and green rolled fondant, and cut discs of each with round cutter. Set aside scraps for making plaque supports. Lay discs on cupcakes, and press gently to secure.

6. Roll remaining orange rolled fondant into a ball and flatten on two sides. Affix on orange cupcake, and affix appropriate plaque (Figure C). Repeat with green and yellow cupcakes.

Lucky Lollipop

Anyone who loves lollipops will be delighted with this design: a lollipop and cupcake, all in one!

A

C

B

D

Materials

Rolled fondant in the following colors:

- 1 ounce (28 grams) purple
- ⅓ ounce (10 grams) pink
- 2½ ounces (70 grams) orange

Water

1 cupcake

1 teaspoon (5 ml) buttercream or other spread

Tools

Rolling pin

1½-inch (3.8 cm) plain round cutter

Lollipop stick

Fine paintbrush

Serrated knife

Small spatula

Spiral rolling pin

3-inch (7.5 cm) plain round cutter

Instructions

Two hours in advance

1. Thickly roll out purple rolled fondant, and cut disc with smaller round cutter. Carefully insert lollipop stick into disc so that it extends like a real lollipop stick (Figure A).

2. Roll pink rolled fondant into a long thin sausage shape (Figure B).

3. Start from center of cupcake, and draw a spiral using water and fine paintbrush. Affix one end of pink sausage shape to center of spiral, and wind sausage shape along spiral shape, pressing down very gently to affix. Set aside to dry for 2 hours.

Assembling cupcake

4. Level top of cupcake, and spread buttercream evenly on top. Roll out orange rolled fondant. Re-roll once using spiral rolling pin (Figure C). Cut disc with larger round cutter. Lay disc on top of cupcake, and press gently to secure.

5. Insert lollipop into center of cupcake (Figure D).

Make sure lollipop stick is removed before cupcake is eaten!

How Old Are You?!

You're never too old (or too young!) to enjoying seeing your birthday in numbers.

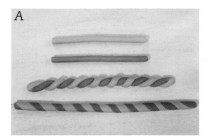

Materials

Number 1

Modeling paste in the following colors:

- 1 ounce (28 grams) purple
- 1 ounce (28 grams) light blue

Number 5

Modeling paste in the following colors:

- 1 ounce (28 grams) pink
- $\frac{1}{10}$ ounce (3 grams) yellow

White royal icing

Cupcake base (per cupcake)

1 cupcake

1 teaspoon (5 ml) buttercream or other spread

Rolled fondant in the following colors:

- 2½ ounces (70 grams) pink
- ⅔ ounce (21 grams) orange

Water

Tools

2-inch (5 cm) green floral wire

Serrated knife

Small spatula

Rolling pin

3-inch (7.5 cm) round cutter

Open-curve crimper

Instructions

Two hours in advance

Number 1

1. Roll blue modeling paste and purple modeling paste into even sausage shapes. Twist sausage shapes together and roll to form a single sausage shape (Figure A).

2. Press wire into bottom of sausage shape, about ⅔ of the way to the top. Gently bend sausage shape at tip of wire to form top part of number. Set aside to dry for 2 hours (Figure B).

Number 5

3. Roll pink modeling paste into a sausage shape. Roll several tiny balls of yellow modeling paste and arrange all over pink sausage shape. Roll gently to inlay. Cut sausage shape into two pieces, taking care that one piece is slightly larger than the other (Figure C).

4. Bend larger piece into a U-shape. Make a shallow cut in middle of smaller piece and bend here at a 90° angle (Figure D). Affix pieces with royal icing. Insert wire on an angle into bottom of number, and set aside to dry for 2 hours.

Assembling cupcake

5. Level top of cupcake, and spread buttercream evenly on top. Roll out pink rolled fondant, and cut disc with round cutter. Lay disc on top of cupcake and press gently to secure. Roll orange rolled fondant into a sausage shape long enough to fit around cupcake. Affix around cupcake; then crimp with open-curve crimper (Figure E).

6. Insert wire extending from number into center of cupcake.

Make sure floral wire is removed before cupcake is eaten!

Here Come the Clowns

Mix and match hats, bowties, eyes, and hairstyles to create a colorful crowd of clowns.

A

C

B

D

Materials

Cupcake base (per cupcake)

1 cupcake

1 teaspoon (15 ml) buttercream or other spread

Rolled fondant in the following colors:

- 2½ ounces (70 grams) skin color
- ⅓ ounce (10 grams) red
- ⅓ ounce (10 grams) white
- Tiny amount yellow
- Tiny amount light blue
- Water

Clown with orange and pink hat

- ½ ounce (14 grams) orange
- ½ ounce (14 grams) pink
- Tiny amount yellow plus 1½ ounces (14 grams)
- ⅒ ounce (3 grams) light blue

Clown with yellow and green hat

- 1 ounce (28 grams) yellow
- ⅒ ounce (3 grams) green
- Tiny amount orange
- ⅒ ounce (3 grams) light blue
- Tiny amount pink

Clown with pink and blue hat

- ½ ounce (14 grams) pink plus a tiny amount
- ½ ounce (14 grams) blue
- Tiny amount orange
- ⅒ ounce (3 grams) light blue
- ½ ounce (14 grams) yellow

Tools

Serrated knife

Small spatula

Rolling pin

3-inch (7.5 cm) round cutter

Instructions

1. Level top of cupcake, and spread buttercream evenly on top. Roll out flesh-colored rolled fondant, and cut disc with round cutter. Lay disc on cupcake and press gently to secure.

2. To make nose, set aside some red rolled fondant for the mouth, and roll the rest into a ball. Flatten slightly and affix in center of cupcake. Divide white rolled fondant in half. Set aside one half for mouth, and shape other half into two even balls for eyes. Flatten balls and affix (Figure A).

3. To make mouth, roll remaining white rolled fondant into a sausage shape, and bend into a crescent. Flatten and affix. Choose one of two types of eye

decorations. To make eyebrows, roll two tiny teardrop shapes of yellow rolled fondant and affix (Figure B). To make eye decorations, roll eight small sausage shapes of yellow rolled fondant and affix in a cross around eyes. Roll tiny balls of light blue rolled fondant and affix on eyes. Roll a thin sausage shape of red rolled fondant and affix in middle of mouth.

Clown with orange and pink hat

4. To make hat, roll out orange rolled fondant. Roll several sausage shapes of pink rolled fondant and lay in diagonal stripes onto orange rolled fondant. Roll gently to inlay; then cut with template on page 124 (Figure C). Roll a tiny amount of yellow rolled fondant into a ball and affix at top. To make bowtie, roll out light blue rolled fondant. Roll several sausage shapes of pink rolled fondant, and lay in stripes on blue rolled fondant. Roll gently to inlay; then cut with template on page 125. To make hair, roll yellow rolled fondant into several elongated teardrop shapes. Affix hat, hair, and bowtie (Figure D). (continued on page 100)

(continued from page 98)

E
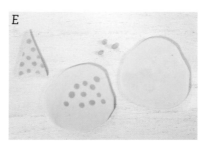

F
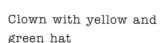

G

H

Clown with yellow and green hat

5. To make hat, roll out half of yellow rolled fondant. Roll several balls of green rolled fondant and arrange on yellow rolled fondant. Roll gently to inlay; then cut with template on page 124 (Figure E). Roll a small ball of orange rolled fondant and affix at top. To make bowtie, roll out blue rolled fondant. Roll several sausage shapes of pink rolled fondant, and lay in stripes on orange rolled fondant. Roll gently to inlay; then cut with template on page 125 (Figure F). Affix hat and bowtie. To make hair, shape remaining yellow rolled fondant into eight larger balls and six smaller balls. Flatten balls and affix around edge of cupcake, taking care to affix smaller balls in front of hat, so as not to conceal it (Figure G).

Clown with pink and blue hat

6. To make hat, roll out ½ ounce (14 grams) pink rolled fondant. Roll several sausage shapes of blue rolled fondant and lay in diagonal strips on pink rolled fondant. Roll gently to inlay; then cut with template on page 124. Roll a small ball of orange rolled fondant and affix at top. To make bowtie, roll out tiny amount pink rolled fondant. Roll several balls of orange rolled fondant and arrange on pink rolled fondant. Roll gently to inlay; then cut with template on page 125. To make hair, roll out yellow rolled fondant and cut with template on page 124. Affix hat, hair, and bowtie (Figure H).

Gallery of Gifts

Most people love to give gifts—these ones come with their own wrapping!

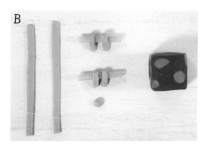

Materials

Red gift

- 1 ounce (28 grams) red
- $\frac{1}{10}$ ounce (3 grams) orange
- $\frac{1}{10}$ ounce (3 grams) light purple

Light yellow gift

- 1 ounce (28 grams) light yellow
- $\frac{1}{10}$ ounce (3 grams) light green
- $\frac{1}{10}$ ounce (3 grams) orange
- Tiny amount light purple

Light pink gift

1 ounce (28 grams) light pink

- $\frac{1}{10}$ ounce (3 grams) light yellow
- $\frac{1}{10}$ ounce (3 grams) orange

Cupcake base (per cupcake)

1 cupcake

- 1 teaspoon (5 ml) buttercream or other spread
- $2\frac{1}{2}$ ounces (70 grams) light green
- $1\frac{1}{3}$ ounces (38 grams) yellow

Water

Tools

Rolling pin

Small sharp knife

Drinking straw

Serrated knife

Small spatula

3-inch (7.5 cm) round cutter

Instructions

One hour in advance

Red gift

1. Roll red rolled fondant into a ball. Roll several small balls of orange rolled fondant and affix all around red ball. Re-roll red ball to inlay orange dots (Figure A). Shape ball into a cube.

2. To make ribbon, set aside a tiny ball of light purple rolled fondant for center, and thinly roll out the rest into a long thin strip. Cut strip into three even pieces. Affix two pieces in a cross on top of gift. Cut third strip into four even pieces. Lay all four pieces on drinking straw so that they take on straw's curve, and set aside to dry for 1 hour (Figure B). When ribbons are completely dry, affix on top of gift. Affix tiny ball in center (Figure C)

Light yellow gift

3. Shape light yellow rolled fondant into a cube (Figure D). Roll out light green rolled fondant into a long thin strip, and cut into two even pieces. Shape orange rolled fondant into seven even teardrops. Roll a tiny ball of light purple rolled fondant (Figure E).

4. Affix light green strips in a cross on top of gift. Affix petals and flower center on top of gift (Figure F).

(continued on page 102)

(continued from page 101)

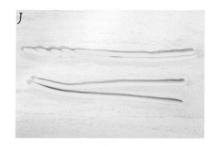

G

J

H

K

I

L

Light pink gift

5. Shape light pink rolled fondant into a cube (Figure G). Roll out light yellow rolled fondant into a long thin strip, and cut into three even pieces. Affix two pieces in a cross on top of gift. Cut third strip into four even pieces and one shorter piece. Lay two longer pieces on drinking straw so that they take on the straw's curve. Twist two other long pieces. Set aside to dry for 1 hour (Figure H).

6. When ribbons are completely dry, affix longer pieces on top of gift. Affix smallest strip over areas where strips are affixed, to conceal.

7. Use the techniques described above and devise your own variations to make a range of colorful gifts (Figure I).

Assembling cupcake

8. Level top of cupcake, and spread buttercream evenly on top. Roll out light green rolled fondant, and cut disc with round cutter. Lay disc on cupcake and press gently to secure.

9. Divide yellow rolled fondant in half and roll each half into a sausage shape long enough to fit around cupcake. Twist sausage shapes together (Figure J), and affix around cupcake (Figure K).

10. Affix one gift to center of each cupcake you make (Figure L).

102

Fun in the Sun

Something Fishy

You don't need bait to catch one of these happy fish; just a little rolled fondant.

A

D

B

E

C

Materials

1 cupcake

1 teaspoon (5 ml) buttercream or other spread

Rolled fondant in the following colors:

• 2½ ounces (70 grams) blue

• ⅙ ounce (5 grams) light blue

• ⅔ ounce (21 grams) green (or color of your choice)

Water

Blue food coloring powder

Tools

Rolling pin

Small sharp knife

3-inch (7.5 cm) round cutter

Bone tool

Toothpick

#6 Pastry tip

Fine paintbrush

Instructions

1. Level top of cupcake, and spread buttercream evenly on top. Roll out blue rolled fondant, and cut disc with round cutter. Lay disc on cupcake and press gently to secure. Make indents for top and bottom of fish using bone tool (Figure A).

2. Roll two thin sausage shapes of light blue rolled fondant, shape into waves, and affix on cupcake. Rub gently with your fingers to inlay (Figure B).

3. To make fish, divide light green rolled fondant in half. Roll one half into a rounded cone. Cut out a wedge for the mouth, and mark eyes with toothpick. Indent scales with wide end of pastry tip (Figure C).

4. To make tail, thickly roll out remaining light green rolled fondant, and cut with template on page 126. Indent scales with pastry tip, and mark lines on tail (Figure D).

5. Affix tail and head to indents. Brush blue food coloring powder onto tip of tail (Figure E).

Perfect Weather

No matter what the weather outside, you'll have plenty of sun at your party with this fabulous threesome.

Materials

3 cupcakes

3 teaspoons (15 ml) buttercream or other spread

Rolled fondant in the following colors:

- 7½ ounces (210 grams) light blue
- 1½ ounces (42 grams) white
- 1 ounce (28 grams) yellow

Water

Tools

Serrated knife

Small spatula

Rolling pin

Small sharp knife

3-inch (7.5 cm) round cutter

Pieces of sponge

Sunshine cutter

Small ball tool

Toothpick

A

C

B

D

Instructions

1. Level tops of cupcakes, and spread buttercream evenly on top. Roll out light blue rolled fondant, and cut three discs with round cutter. Save the scraps for the eyes. Lay one disc on each cupcake and press gently to secure.

2. Thickly roll out white rolled fondant and cut three clouds using template on page 126 (Figure A). Affix one cloud on one cupcake and two clouds on another cupcake. On cupcake with two clouds, allow one cloud to hang over edge, supported until dry by a piece of sponge (Figure B).

3. Roll out yellow rolled fondant and cut with sunshine cutter (Figure C).

4. Mark large circle for face, and make moon-shaped cuts for smile and cheeks. To make nose, roll a tiny ball of yellow rolled fondant, and affix. Indent eyes with ball tool. Roll two tiny balls with light blue fondant, and affix. Mark center of eyes with toothpick (Figure D).

Bathing Beauty

This bikini is always the right size!

A

C

B

D

Materials

1 cupcake

1 teaspoon (5 ml) buttercream or other spread

Rolled fondant in the following colors:

• 2½ ounces (70 grams) flesh-colored

• ⅔ ounce (21 grams) red

• ⅒ ounce (3 grams) orange

• Tiny amount yellow

• Tiny amount pink

Water

Tools

Serrated knife

Small spatula

Rolling pin

3-inch (7.5 cm) round cutter

Toothpick

Design wheeler

Small flower cutter

Instructions

1. Level top of cupcake, and spread buttercream evenly on top. Roll out flesh-colored rolled fondant, and cut disc with round cutter. Lay disc on cupcake and press gently to secure. Mark belly button with toothpick near center of cupcake.

2. Thinly roll out half of red rolled fondant, and cut bikini bottom using template on page 127 (Figure A). Affix bottom onto cupcake, and make seams using design wheeler (Figure B).

3. Thinly roll out remaining red rolled fondant and cut bikini top using template on page 127 (Figure C). Roll scraps into thin sausage shapes for straps. Affix bikini top and straps, and make seams using design wheeler.

4. Divide orange rolled fondant in half and roll each half into a thin strip. Affix strips along top of bikini bottom, and bottom of bikini top.

5. Roll out yellow rolled fondant, and cut flower using flower cutter. Affix flower to top left corner of bikini top. Roll a tiny ball of pink rolled fondant, and affix in flower center (Figure D).

You're a Lifesaver

No need to wait for an emergency to make this fabulous cupcake.

A

C

B

D

Materials

1 cupcake

1 teaspoon (5 ml) buttercream or other spread

Rolled fondant in the following colors:

- 1½ ounces (42 grams) dark blue
- ⅔ ounce (21 grams) turquoise
- ⅔ ounce (21 grams) red-orange
- ⅓ ounce (10 grams) white

Water

Tools

Serrated knife

Small spatula

Rolling pin

3-inch (7.5 cm) fluted round cutter

Clay gun

Instructions

1. Level top of cupcake, and spread buttercream evenly on top. Shape dark blue rolled fondant into four thick sausage shapes. Shape turquoise rolled fondant into three thin sausage shapes. Press sausage shapes together in an alternating pattern; then carefully roll out to make a streaked sheet of rolled fondant. Cut disc with fluted round cutter (Figure A). Lay disc on cupcake and press gently to secure.

2. Roll red-orange rolled fondant into a long thick sausage shape. Flatten ends and bring together to form a ring. Affix ends (Figure B).

3. To make rope, fill clay gun with white rolled fondant, and squeeze to produce a long thin rope shape. Twist to form a rope that is at least twice as long as ring's circumference (Figure C).

4. Affix ring onto center of cupcake. Cut rope in half and wrap one half around cupcake. Cut other half into four even pieces, and fold each piece in half. Lay one doubled-up rope over ring seam to conceal it. Lay other three doubled ropes at even internals all around ring (Figure D).

Beach Umbrella

Keep your cool when the heat is on with this design.

A

B

C

D

Materials

Modeling paste in the following colors:

- 1½ ounces (42 grams) dark blue
- ½ ounce (14 grams) white

Rolled fondant in the following colors:

- Small amount white
- 1¼ ounces (36 grams) light blue
- 1¼ ounces (36 grams) sand
- ⅙ ounce (5 grams) very light blue

Water

1 cupcake

1 teaspoon (5 ml) buttercream or other spread

Tools

Rolling pin

3½-inch (9 cm) round cutter

Small sharp knife

1-inch (2.5 cm) round cutter

Lollipop stick

Small plastic ball, cut in half

Serrated knife

Small spatula

3-inch (7.5 cm) round cutter

Instructions

Six hours in advance

1. Roll out blue modeling paste. Thinly roll out white modeling paste, and cut disc with largest round cutter. Cut disk into eight even sections. Affix four sections onto sheet of blue modeling paste, leaving even spaces between each section (Figure A).

2. Roll gently to inlay; then cut disc with largest round cutter. Shape circumference of disc by removing eye-shaped pieces of rolled fondant from edge of each section using smallest round cutter (Figure B).

3. Poke hole in center of umbrella with lollipop stick; then press umbrella inside plastic ball half, so that decorated side of umbrella is flush with ball. Set aside to dry for 6 hours (Figure C).

4. When umbrella is dry, roll a small ball of white rolled fondant and place inside umbrella, just below hole. Insert lollipop stick through ball and hole, so that top of stick extends through top of umbrella (Figure D). Press a small cone of white rolled fondant onto stick poking through top of umbrella, to secure.

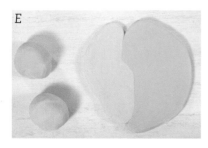

E

F

G

Assembling cupcake

5. Level top of cupcake, and spread buttercream evenly on top. Place light blue rolled fondant and sand rolled fondant side-by-side and roll out, so that colors are connected (Figure E). Cut disc with medium round cutter. Lay disc on top of cupcake and press gently to secure.

6. Roll three small sausage shapes of very light blue rolled fondant, and place on sea side of cupcake. Rub gently with your fingers to inlay (Figure F). Insert lollipop in sandy side of cupcake (Figure G).

Make sure lollipop stick is removed before cupcake is eaten!

Templates

Collar (Smiling Mom, page 16)

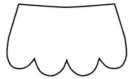

Bowtie (Delighted Dad, page 18)

Collar (Boy Oh Boy!, page 20)

Hair (Boy Oh Boy!, page 20)

Hair (Girl of Your Dreams, page 22)

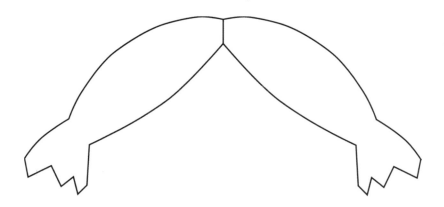

Paper Triangles (Elegant Paper Waves, page 36)

Treetop (Springtime Blossoms, page 48)

Teeth (Pink Monster, page 58)

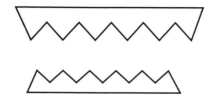

Eyes (Mischievous Monkey, page 66)

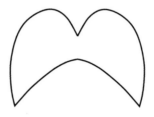

Eyes patch × 2 (Positively Panda, page 74)

2 ×

Plaques (Say It with Cupcakes!, page 92)

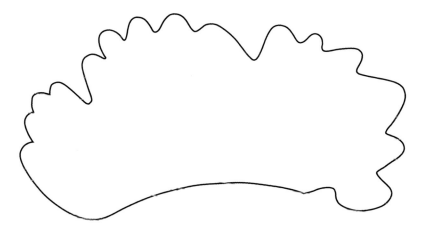

Plaques (Say It with Cupcakes!, page 92)

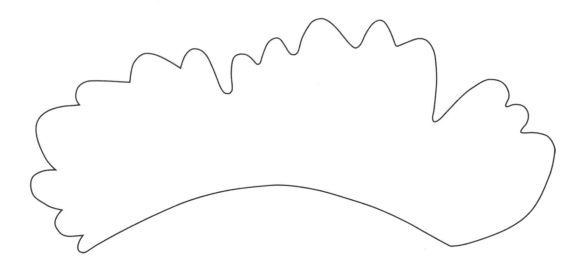

Plaques (Say It with Cupcakes!, page 92)

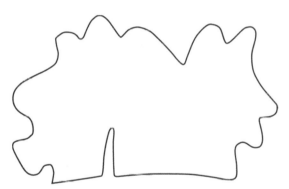

Hat (Here Come the Clowns!, page 98)

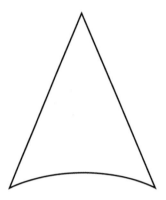

Hair (Here Come the Clowns!, page 98)

2 ×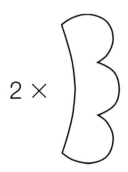

Bowtie (Here Come the Clowns!, page 98)

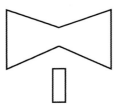

Fishtail (Something Fishy, page 106)

Clouds (Perfect Weather, page 108)

Bikini (Bathing Beauty, page 110)

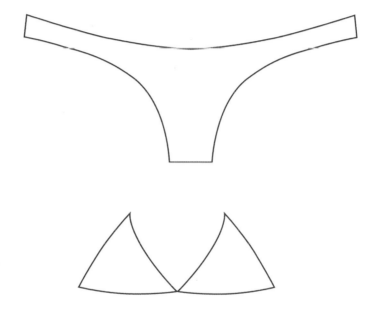

Index

B

Baby Booty 82
Baby Face 86
baking cups 12
ball tools 12
Bathing Beauty 110
Beach Umbrella 114
Bear on Bib 84
Big-Hearted Cupcake 32
Blue Monster 52
bone tools 12
Boy Oh Boy! 20
buttercream 8

C

Celebrate in Silver 28
chocolate cupcakes 7
clay gun 12
Cute as a Bunny 78
cutters 12

D

Dainty Daisy 40
decorating bags and tips 12
Delighted Dad 18
design wheelers 12
Doggone It! 24
drinking straws 12
dry spaghetti 13

E

Elegant Paper Waves 36

F

Field of Flowers 46
floral wire 12
food coloring pens 12
Freshly Picked Flower 44

G

Gallery of Gifts 101
gel food color, adding 10
Girl of Your Dreams 22
Green Monster 54

H

Heart-to-Heart 30
Here Come the Clowns 98
How Old Are You?! 96

K

knives 13

L

lollipop sticks 12
Lovable Lion 68
Lucky Lollipop 94

M

Miniature Wedding Cake 34
Mischievous Monkey 66
modeling paste 8

O

open-curve crimper 13
Orange Monster 60

P

Pacifier, Please 80
paintbrushes 13
Perfect Weather 108
Pink Monster 58
pizza cutters 13
plastic wrap 13
Positively Panda 74
Private Garden 42
Purple Monster 56

R

ribbon 13
rolled fondant 8
rolling pins 13
royal icing 8

S

Say It with Cupcakes! 92
small spatulas 13
Smiling Mom 16
Something Fishy 106
sponge 13
Springtime Blossoms 48

T

Teddy Bear 88
templates 117
Tiger's Tale 72
tools and materials 12
toothpicks 13

V

Very Happy Hippo 70

W

white cupcakes 7
wooden skewers 13

Y

Yellow Monster 62
You're a Lifesaver 112